Portfoolio 8

The Year in Canadian Caricature

EDITED BY GUY BADEAUX
TEXT BY CHARLES GORDON   FOREWORD BY JOSH FREED

MACMILLAN CANADA
TORONTO, ONTARIO CANADA

© The Association of Canadian Editorial Cartoonists 1992
   Raeside cartoons © Raeside 1992

Canadian Cataloguing in Publication Data

The National Library of Canada has catalogued this title as follows:

Portfoolio 8: The Year in Canadian Caricature

Annual.
Description based on: 87.
The letters "oo" in the title are formed by the first digit of date, 85-
ISSN 0839-6485
ISBN 0-7715-9184-5 (1992)

1. Canada - Politics and government - 1984- -
Caricatures and cartoons. 2. World politics -
Caricatures and cartoons. 3. Canadian wit and humor, Pictorial.

NC1300-P67   971.064'7'0267   C89-030416-5

Macmillan Canada
A Division of Canada Publishing Corporation
Toronto, Ontario, Canada

Printed in Canada

Design: **Mathilde Hébert**
Front Cover Cartoon: **Brian Gable**; colour by **Gité**
Back Cover Cartoon: **Dan Murphy**

BADO, *Le Droit*, Ottawa, February 7, 1991

NNA 1991 FINALISTS

GABLE, *The Globe and Mail*, September 7, 1991

LARTER, *The Edmonton Sun*, November 6, 1991

FOREWORD

This is your nation's 125th birthday but you're not exactly popping open the champagne. It's been a long, bleak year and you are one confused Canadian, like the cartoon in this book of a beaver on a psychiatrist's couch. If you're a westerner you wonder why Quebec is distinct rather than unique, special, unusual, particular, eccentric or atypically singular — and why you're not. If you're a Quebecer you wonder why the West needs five senators for every three people; if you're a Maritimer you wonder why there are three people for every job.

No matter what part of Canada you are from, you're weary of words. You have been battered by briefs, paralyzed by polls, crushed by constitutional chatter; you feel trapped in a confederation of words. But cheer up — you are holding the antidote. This book has very few words, just very funny caricatures that capture the past year in a way words never could.

A meeting of "Constitutional Junkies Anonymous" (Hi, I'm Bob and I'm an asymmetrical federalist). Ottawa riot police dispersing a crowd by reading out constitutional amendments, as deadly as tear gas. A post free-trade map of North America where Mexico is a "manufacturing" zone, the U.S. is a "retail" zone and Canada is reserved for "parking".

There is John Crosbie at a "fish and chips" stand — with no fish; Eric Lindros, "boy blunder" of the NHL; " Sergeant" Claude Morin of the RCMP and a cast of others who will make you chuckle at being Canuck, regardless of your language or constitutional colour.

I sometimes think words may be the only obstacle to our country's harmony, that Canadians get along well with one another as long as we don't talk about it. All we need is a committee of caricaturists to draw up a plan for Canada, a coast-to-coast cartoon constitution that has no clauses to quibble over, no words to debate, no veto to veto.

So see this volume as a draft document: a white paper on Canada saying more about your country in fewer words than anything else you've paid for this year. And lean back and enjoy the silence. You've earned it.

Josh Freed

The Constitution
Saving the country wasn't easy

By the time you read this, the country will have been saved and its people will be in the process of living happily ever after. Unfortunately, because there is a lag time in publishing — between the time this book is completed and it reaches your hands — we are unable to provide cartoons celebrating the successful completion of a constitutional agreement. So we're sorry for that, but we can imagine what it will be like: people smiling and laughing from coast to coast, Westerners slapping Quebeckers on the back and congratulating them on their distinctness; native people joyfully practising self-government without bothering any provincial jurisdictions; and, above all, the Triple-E Senate, working to perfection, equally, electedly, and effectively.

Knowing all this as well as you do, you will have to use your imagination and cast your mind back to a sadder and more confused time, the time when the cartoons prepared for this book were drawn. In those days, Canadians were not happy. They had been through the Spicer, Castonguay-Dobbie and Beaudoin-Dobbie committees. They had seen coast-to-coast unity conferences, referendum scares.

They were sick of the whole thing back in those days, not happy and proud the way they undoubtedly are now, as you read these words. People snoozed in front of the TV news, disappeared from public spaces when words about the constitution were heard — distinct society, Triple-E Senate, native self-government.

Those were the issues, although it is probably hard to remember them in these days of euphoria.

It is probably also hard to remember the cast of characters. Remember Joe Clark when he was a mere Unity minister? Remember Ovide Mercredi, Don Getty — wasn't he great when he did his Preston Manning impression? Jacques Parizeau — does anybody remember Jacques Parizeau, who thought the constitutional crisis was going to drive the country apart instead of bring it together as never before. Parizeau was so convinced he was right that he travelled down to the United States, just to get the people there used to the idea of him representing a sovereign nation.

Robert Bourassa, who will undoubtedly be seen as a national hero by the time this book is out, was often seen by cartoonists as an equivocating sort of person, even an opportunist. And Brian Mulroney was still seen as a schemer, a roller of dice, instead of hailed as the constitutional statesman we know him as today.

It just goes to show how times can change.

(Note to editor: If times don't change, and in the unlikely event that all of the country's problems are not solved by November, please replace this with the piece on why the constitutional talks were never going to work anyway.)

CANADIAN CROWD CONTROL

GABLE, *The Globe and Mail*

CANADA

GABLE, *The Globe and Mail*

New offers

DELATRI, *Le Nouvelliste*, Trois-Rivières

MOU, *The Daily News*, Halifax

CUMMINGS, *The Winnipeg Free Press*

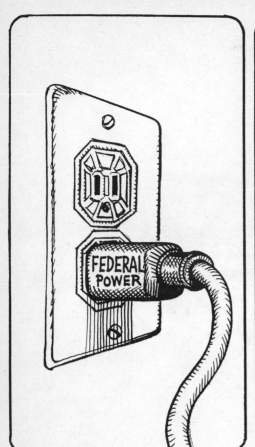
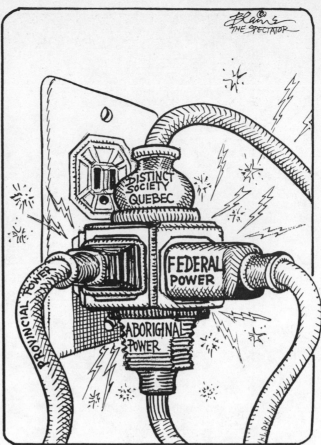

BLAINE, *The Spectator*, Hamilton

RODEWALT, *The Calgary Herald*

LARTER, *The Calgary Sun*

DEWAR, *The Ottawa Sun*

DELATRI, *Le Nouvelliste*, Trois-Rivières

1. Stinks
2. Distinct
3. Distinctive, but pushing their luck.

HEY KIDS! MATCH THE ICON TO THE APPROPRIATE WORD.

JENKINS, *The Globe and Mail*

RODEWALT, *The Calgary Herald*

RODEWALT, *The Calgary Herald*

RAESIDE, *The Times-Colonist*, Victoria

RODEWALT, *The Calgary Herald*

HARROP, *The Globe and Mail*

KING, *The Ottawa Citizen*

AISLIN, *The Gazette / The Toronto Star*

"... MY NAME IS BOB, AND I'M AN ASYMMETRICAL FEDERALIST'..."

GABLE, *The Globe and Mail*

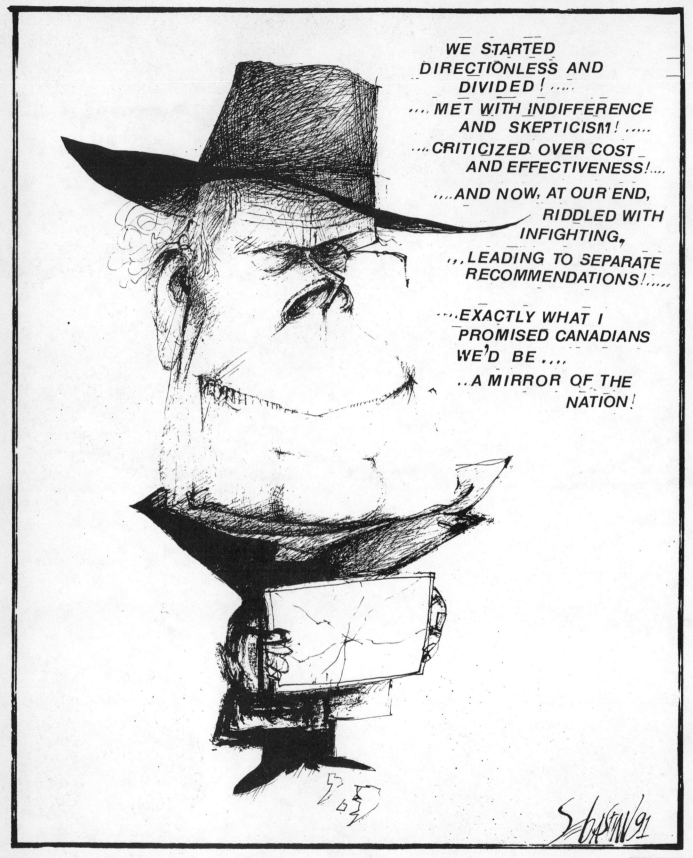

SEBASTIAN

NEASE, *The Oakville Beaver*

COMMISSIONNITES :

BÉLANGER - CAMPEAU   SPICER   CASTONGUAY - DOBBIE

Commissionnitis:
— We have taken the temperature of the people!
— I have done likewise

GARNOTTE

.21

ONE SMALL STEP FOR CANADA, ONE GIANT LEAP FOR CONFEDERATION.

JENKINS, *The Globe and Mail*

BADO, *Le Droit*, Ottawa

ANDY, *Toronto Sun*

SAUER, *Le Devoir*

The official portrait of Canada's latest national unity committee

AISLIN, *The Gazette / The Toronto Star*

This could take longer than I thought...

BADO, *Le Droit*, Ottawa

BADO, *Le Droit*, Ottawa

How to get rid of the Dobbie-Castonguay committee.

PIER, *Le Journal de Montréal*

RODEWALT, *The Calgary Herald*

PRITCHARD

MURPHY, *The Province*, Vancouver

AISLIN, *The Gazette / The Toronto Star*

DONATO, *The Toronto Sun*

CONSTITUTIONAL FINISH LINE

SENATE REFORM

JOE

MAYES, *The Edmonton Journal*

...WELL, WE SHOULD HAVE THE CONSTITUTION DONE ANY DAY NOW...

...EH?

MALLETTE, *The Financial Post*

.31

SEBASTIAN

PIER, *Le Journal de Montréal*

MALLETTE, *The Financial Post*

PRITCHARD

SEBASTIAN

MOU, *The Daily News*, Halifax

PETERSON, *The Vancouver Sun*

MURPHY, *The Province*, Vancouver

LARTER, *The Calgary Sun*

SEE JACQUES. SEE JACQUES RUN.

JENKINS, *The Globe and Mail*

S TILL ANGRY OVER THE INCIDENT AT THE LAKE...

...LITTLE BOUBOU LOCKED HIMSELF IN THE CLOSET AND REFUSED TO COME OUT...

TODD

CONSTITUTION

SAUER, *Le Devoir*

DEWAR, *The Ottawa Sun*

POSITIONS CONSTITUTIONNELLES...

GARNOTTE, *Nouvelles CSN*

PIER, *Le Journal de Montréal*

GODIN, *Voir*, Montreal

MALLETTE, *The Financial Post*

HOGAN, *The Moncton Times-Transcript*

CONSTITUTIONAL MR. FIX-IT.

JENKINS, *The Globe and Mail*

TRIPLE E:

- EDMONTON
- ESKIMO
- ÉPAIS

BADO, *Le Droit*, Ottawa

.43

DON GETTY'S
NEW BRAIN —

CUMMINGS, *The Winnipeg Free Press*

GETTY CALLS FOR
END TO OFFICIAL
BILINGUALISM

...DID **MY** LIPS MOVE ?..

EDWARDS, *The Whig-Standard*, Kingston

AISLIN, *The Gazette / The Toronto Star*

PRITCHARD

...NO THANKS...I HATE FRENCH DRESSING...

GABLE, *The Globe and Mail*

The Economy
Misery loves companies

Every year there is something different happening in the Canadian economy. That is what makes it so much fun to watch, although not so much fun to live in, unless you are a cartoonist.

However, if you were a cartoonist, you would have to spend all your time drawing misery, which would surely get to you after a while. There is only so much misery you can take.

The new stuff this time was the strike by the Public Service Alliance of Canada, which proved that Ottawa is not necessarily Fat City — at least not if you happen to be working in certain government jobs there. Despite the strike, the country seemed to carry on as inefficiently as ever, which says something about the resiliency of our national institutions.

The other new thing was the beautifully cartoonable streak of cruelty in the federal budget, in which it was decided that the way to solve Canada's economic problems was to throw people out of work.

True, this had been government policy for several years, but now people in the government were being thrown out of work. Before, you had to work in a factory or something.

On an entirely unrelated matter, the GST continued, more entrenched than most parts of our constitution, yet without requiring any time-consuming and cumbersome negotiations with the provinces.

And on another entirely unrelated matter, free trade continued, working so well at throwing people out of work that there was talk of moving it into Mexico, where apparently not enough industries are closing.

Canada's interest in free trade with Mexico is clear: when free trade causes companies to leave Mexico, some of them may wind up here.

WHAT THE FEDS GAVE MANAGEMENT FOR TURNING UP TO WORK...

WHAT THE FEDS ARE GIVING EMPLOYEES FOR GOING BACK TO WORK...

RAESIDE, *The Times-Colonist*, Victoria

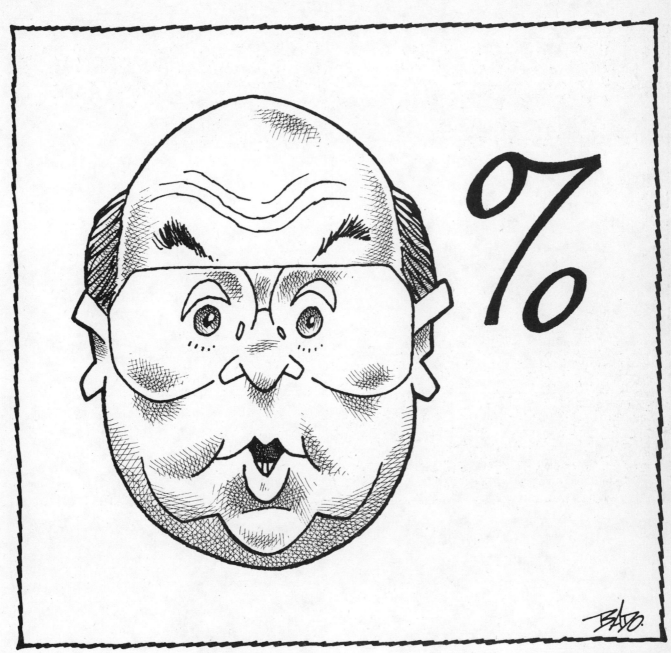

BADO, *Le Droit*, Ottawa

NEWS ITEM : Motorcycles one of few items cheaper after one year of the G.S.T.

CONSTABLE, *Union Art Services*

MACKINNON, *The Chronicle-Herald*, Halifax

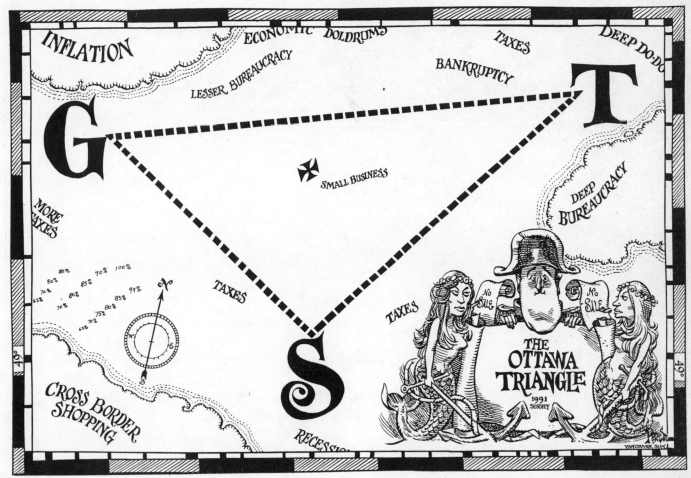

PETERSON, *The Vancouver Sun*

DELATRI, *Le Nouvelliste*, Trois-Rivières

KRIEGER, *The Province*, Vancouver

TING, *The London Free Press*

KING, *The Ottawa Citizen*

CORRIGAN, *The Toronto Star*

POWER STEERING —

CUMMINGS, *The Winnipeg Free Press*

CONSTABLE, *Union Art Services*

RAESIDE, *The Times-Colonist*, Victoria

PRITCHARD

LA POSITION DU CANADA
AU GATT...

Canada's position at the Gatt...

— We're hanging in!

GARNOTTE, *Nouvelles CSN*

BLAINE, *The Spectator*, Hamilton

KRIEGER, *The Province*, Vancouver

LARTER, *The Calgary Sun*

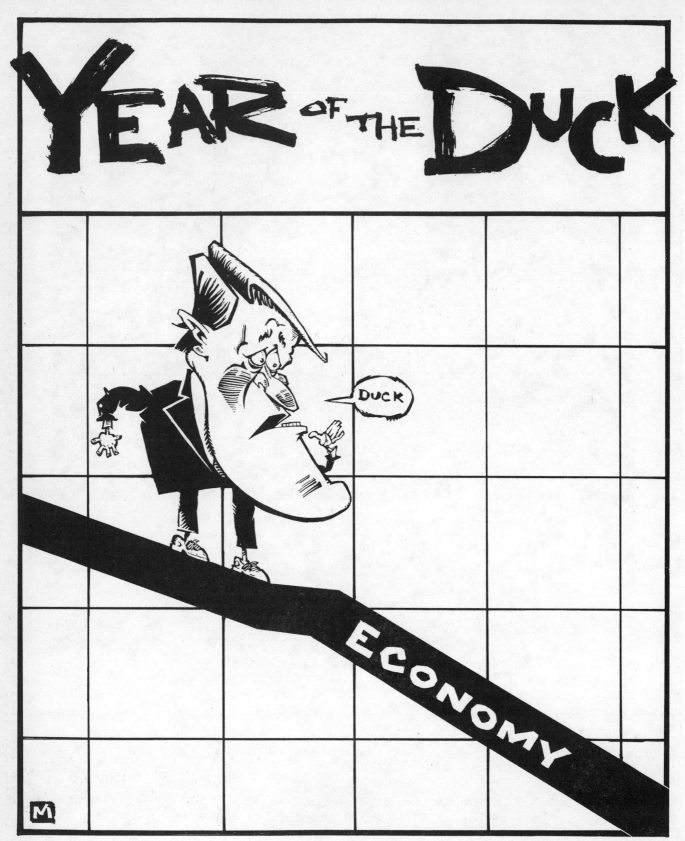

MURPHY, *The Province*, Vancouver

PETERSON, *The Vancouver Sun*

WICKS, *Southam News Syndicate*

PRITCHARD

CONSTABLE, *Union Art Services*

SEBASTIAN

PETERSON, *The Vancouver Sun*

ANDY, *Financial Times*

IT JUST KEEPS GOING AND GOING....

MAYES, *The Edmonton Journal*

WICKS, *Southam News Syndicate*

KING, *The Ottawa Citizen*

BEUTEL, *The Telegraph-Journal*, Saint John

NEASE, *The Oakville Beaver*

BADO, *Le Droit*, Ottawa

MACKINNON, *The Chronicle-Herald*, Halifax

RODEWALT, *The Calgary Herald*

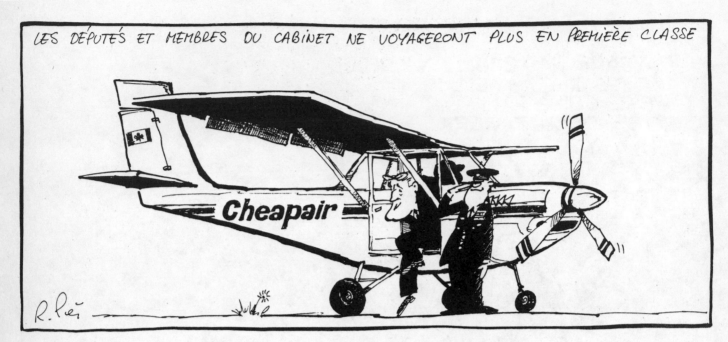

MPs and cabinet ministers will no longer travel first class.

PIER, *Le Journal de Montréal*

HOGAN, *The Moncton Times-Transcript*

PETERSON, *The Vancouver Sun*

Great Canadian Issues
We should stick to hockey

As always, there are those transcendent moments, those great issues that define us as Canadians. It's too bad about that, but there it is. Other nations face war and famine, revolution and erupting volcanoes. We have a hockey players' strike in which it is argued, with a straight face by the players, that several hundred thousand dollars a season is not enough for a season, and, by the owners, that they can barely make ends meet and would probably get out of hockey and into some much more profitable line of work if it were not for their intense loyalty and profound sense of duty to the fans. Hockey also has an HIV-positive woman who claims to have known many players. Volcanoes can be more fun.

Another transcendent issue was the hot rumour that the prime minister would cease being the prime minister and become the secretary-general of the United Nations. Canadians had a hard time figuring out where their heads were at on this one. As Canadians and as long-time supporters of the UN, they would be proud to have one of their own holding that distinguished and powerful position. But, on the other hand, were they just saying that so they could get someone else as prime minister?

And what of the man himself, who said he wasn't running for the job, but neglected to scratch his name off the unofficial list of candidates until the whole nation was in a frenzy either over his leaving or his staying, and the whole world was in a frenzy trying to figure out whether it was a good thing to have a secretary-general whose former constituents seemed so eager to give him up to the world. Eventually, the prime minister decided to stay and the rest is history, or will be sooner or later.

Then there was the fuss over the Great Whale development in Quebec. In case it never rises, you will remember it as the one where people who always complain about Canadian decisions being made in the United States were just delighted that New York State decided not to buy Quebec hydro-electric power, thus scuttling the project.

It is probably just as well that we devote so much of our time to hockey. Other issues seem to confuse us,

RECENT CONSUMER POLLING INDICATES THAT A PROPOSED COMMEMORATIVE MULRONEY STAMP IS UNMARKETABLE....

...14% WERE PREPARED TO LICK THE BACK SIDE... BUT 86% INSISTED ON SPITTING ON THE FRONT

TODD

DONATO, *The Toronto Sun*

CORRIGAN, *The Toronto Star*

POLLBEARERS.

MAYES, *The Edmonton Journal*

HARROP, *The Globe and Mail*

JENKINS, *The Globe and Mail*

LEFCOURT

SEBASTIAN

PETERSON, *The Vancouver Sun*

CANADIAN FOREPLAY

MACKINNON, *The Chronicle-Herald*, Halifax

THEN SUDDENLY IT DAWNED ON BILLY... ALL THIS TIME HE'D HAD IN HIS HANDS
THE POWER TO MAKE OR BREAK THE NHL PLAYERS ASSOCIATION...

KING, *The Ottawa Citizen*

CEPELLA, *The Nelson Daily News*

MACKINNON, *The Chronicle-Herald*, Halifax

MAYES, *The Edmonton Journal*

LAF

GODIN, *Voir*, Montreal

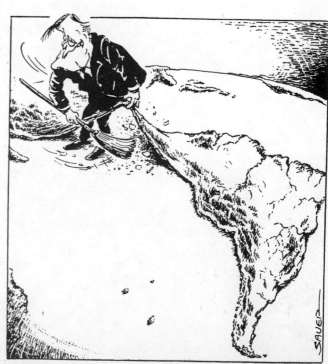

SAUER, *Le Devoir*

PRITCHARD

GABLE, *The Globe and Mail*

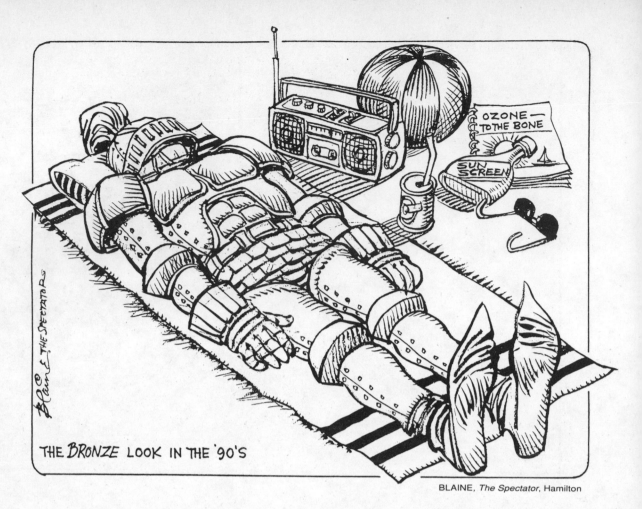

THE *BRONZE* LOOK IN THE '90'S

BLAINE, *The Spectator*, Hamilton

PIER, *Le Journal de Montréal*

OLSON, *The Vancouver Courier*

KING, *The Ottawa Citizen*

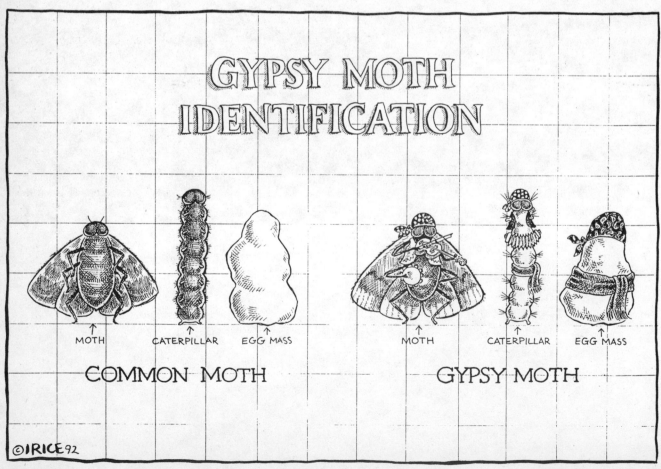

RICE, *The Vancouver Sun*

KING, *The Ottawa Citizen*

KING, *The Ottawa Citizen*

PRITCHARD

NEASE, *The Oakville Beaver*

The Provinces
A jest of cod

Out in the provinces, away from the cares of the world, away from all cares but the Triple-E Senate, the Distinct Society, native self-government, and what was that other thing again? — out in the provinces the premiers laboured away, getting elected, getting defeated, selling out, going to court, and generally presiding over some of the worst economic times anyone has ever seen.

The only thing worse than being a premier would be being a farmer or a fisherman or someone trying to make a living by working. Not that being a politician was terrifically easy. You try to do a simple business deal while in office and look what happens: people yell at you all across British Columbia; the ones who aren't yelling are laughing, and the ones who aren't laughing are voting NDP.

On the other hand, you could be in Ontario, deciding that maybe you shouldn't be dogmatic about putting in NDP policies, this being a recession and all. You try to keep the deficit from getting out of control. So what does that get you? People yelling at you for selling out. Then you do a budget that looks more like the kind of thing a New Democrat might do, and what happens? People yell at you for being dogmatic and running up a big deficit. And then, being a friend of labour, you get to preside over back-to-work legislation when Toronto transit workers go on strike. You could be having more fun, but then you'd be in opposition. You could be having less fun, but then you'd be in Newfoundland, trying to fish.

DEWAR, *The Ottawa Sun*

BLAINE, *The Spectator*, Hamilton

GABLE, *The Globe and Mail*

WICKS, *Southam News Syndicate*

CUMMINGS, *The Winnipeg Free Press*

GOOD EVENING. THE WEST EDMONTON MALL IS BEING SUED BY DISNEY OVER THE USE OF THE NAME 'FANTASYLAND'

A SPOKESMAN FOR DISNEY SAID THAT THE NAME IS THEIRS ALONE AND CANNOT BE USED BY ANYONE FOR ANY PURPOSE WHATSOEVER.

FIVE TO ONE THEY LEARN ABOUT BOB RAE'S DEFICIT AND COME DOWN HARD ON 'TOMORROWLAND'!

HARROP, *The Globe and Mail*

KING, *The Ottawa Citizen*

RAESIDE, *The Times-Colonist*, Victoria

MURPHY, *The Province*, Vancouver

PETERSON, *The Vancouver Sun*

THE SOCREDS TOP 10 REASONS FOR LOSING THE ELECTION...

1. THE NDP
2. THE MEDIA
3. UNINFORMED VOTERS...
4. THE LIBERALS
5. VANDER ZALM
6. AWKWARD COURT CASES
7. MARTIANS
8. SANTA CLAUS
9. IT WAS THURSDAY. OCTOBER 17 Thurs.
10. EXCESS GAMMA RAYS

RAESIDE, *The Times-Colonist*, Victoria

KRIEGER, *The Province*, Vancouver

GABLE, *The Globe and Mail*

MAYES, *The Edmonton Journal*

EDWARDS, *The Whig-Standard*, Kingston

BEUTEL, *The Telegraph-Journal*, Saint John

EAST COAST STILL LIFE

HIBERNIA

CUMMINGS, *The Winnipeg Free Press*

Fossil Fuel

HIBERNIA

GABLE, *The Globe and Mail*

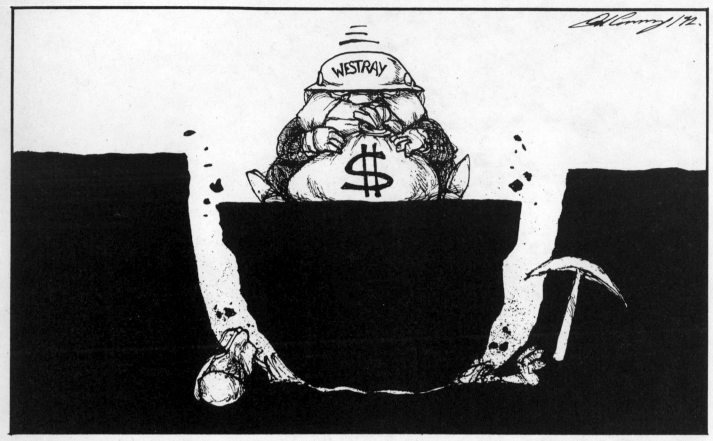

CUMMINGS, *The Winnipeg Free Press*

News item: Governments poured more than $100 million into doomed Nova Scotia mine

AISLIN, *The Gazette / The Toronto Star*

The World
Bedtime for Bosnia

This was the year you really had to pay attention. Countries you'd never heard of, because they weren't countries a year ago, were all of a sudden warring with other countries you'd never heard of because they weren't countries either. That made it tough. Where was Bosnia? Who were the good guys — or were there good guys at all?

That's another thing that made it tough — the absence of the Evil Empire. In the old days, if you wanted to know which side had the good guys on it, it was the one that the Evil Empire wasn't supporting — or vice versa, if you happened to be an Evil Empire fan or someone who, unaccountably, didn't always agree with Ronald Reagan.

Anyway, the Evil Empire went, as you know if you read your Portfoolio last year. And the big hero, the man who brought democracy to Eastern Europe, who got the Evil out of the Empire, was Gorbachev. You knew that because he was on all the magazine covers. That was very good. It was a heroic story, a good story and one we could all understand without reading up on things too much.

What happened next wasn't so good, if we interpret it correctly. The Evil Empire broke up (good), but it broke up too much (bad). It wasn't evil (good) and it wasn't an empire (also good), but each country in the former empire turned out to be many countries and they all wanted to be independent (maybe good), like Yugoslavia (bad).

Worse, there was nothing to eat.

That, in a nutshell, is how Yeltsin took over. If your grandchildren ask you, that's what happened. Meanwhile, Gorby did what all formerly powerful people do: he disappeared and became a consultant. Any day now he will turn up, helping the Burger King people get a choice location in Red Square. This is the democratic way of doing things.

Of course, in the established democracies of the world, such as the United States and Canada, there were no such troubles. There was only the problem of policemen getting away with murder, or seeming to, and rioters getting away with VCRs. In this respect, the citizens of Toronto showed that they would not take a back seat to the citizens of Los Angeles, except in the area of killing people. Canadians still lag in that area, but we can break windows with the best of them.

CUMMINGS, *The Winnipeg Free Press*

PETERSON, *The Vancouver Sun*

LARTER, *The Calgary Sun*

CUMMINGS, *The Winnipeg Free Press*

CURATOLO, *The Edmonton Sun*

SEBASTIAN

PRITCHARD

BLAINE, *The Spectator*, Hamilton

CORRIGAN, *The Toronto Star*

AISLIN, *The Gazette / The Toronto Star*

EDWARDS, *The Whig-Standard*, Kingston

ANDY, *Toronto Sun*

SAUER, *Le Devoir*

CUMMINGS, *The Winnipeg Free Press*

THERE IT IS, PLAINLY VISIBLE IN THE OPENING...SEE THAT YELLOWISH TINGE? SCALPEL!

I'M GOING IN...THEEERE WE GO, NO PROBLEM. FORCEPS!

GOT IT! HIS **GOLD CARD!** NOW LET'S CLOSE UP THE WALLET!

BOY, IS THIS GUY LUCKY! HE'D BE A GONER UP IN CANADA!

OLSON, *The Vancouver Courier*

CORRIGAN, *The Toronto Star*

PRITCHARD

MURPHY, *The Province*, Vancouver

AISLIN, *The Gazette / The Toronto Star*

The Statue of Lobotomy

KING, *The Ottawa Citizen*

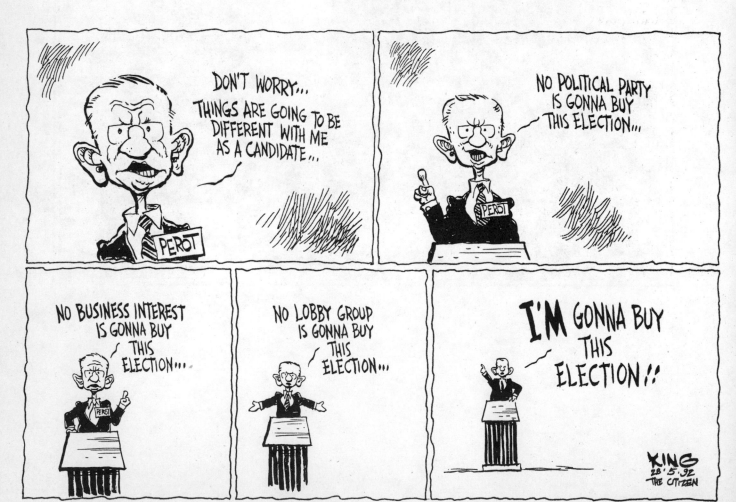

KING, *The Ottawa Citizen*

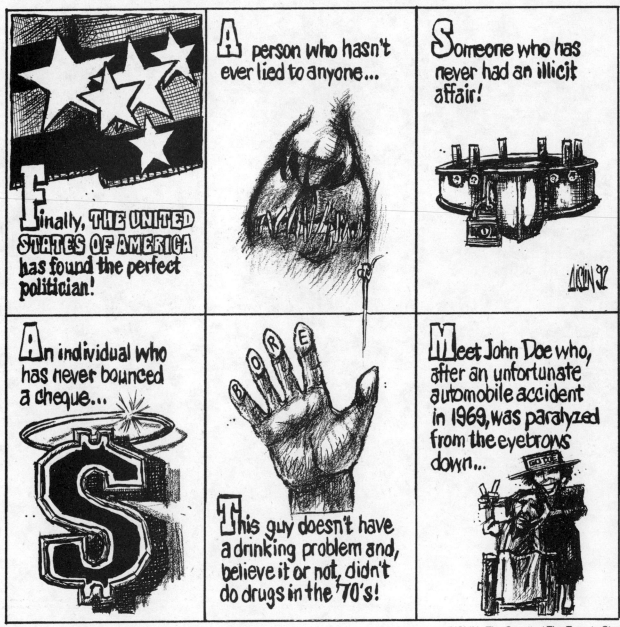

AISLIN, *The Gazette / The Toronto Star*

KING, *The Ottawa Citizen*

the Pro-family Ticket:

SEBASTIAN

KING, *THE OTTAWA CITIZEN*

RAESIDE, *The Times-Colonist*, Victoria

GABLE, *The Globe and Mail*

NEASE, *The Oakville Beaver*

WICKS, *Southam News Syndicate*

AISLIN, *The Gazette / The Toronto Star*

RAESIDE, *The Times-Colonist*, Victoria

MURPHY, *The Province*, Vancouver

ANDY, *Miller Features Syndicate*

PETERSON, *The Vancouver Sun*

LARTER, *The Calgary Sun*

BADO, *Le Droit*, Ottawa

ANDY, *Toronto Sun*

CUMMINGS, *The Winnipeg Free Press*

DEWAR, *The Ottawa Sun*

GABLE, *The Globe and Mail*

MAYES, *The Edmonton Journal*

MACKINNON, *The Chronicle-Herald*, Halifax

OLSON, *The Vancouver Courier*

DONATO, *The Toronto Sun*

NEASE, *The Oakville Beaver*

KING, *The Ottawa Citizen*

DEWAR OTTAWA SUN

People
Stop the kaleidoscope, I want to get off

A kaleidoscope of personalities flashes across the world stage. A kaleidoscope probably can't flash; it can't do anything, actually, unless you hold it to your eye, point it at the light and twist it. But you get the idea. A year that has Mordecai Richler disturbing the peace, Eric Lindros disturbing the hockey establishment, the Reichmann brothers disturbing the bankers, and Roberta Bondar disturbing the heavens can't be all dull.

Claude Morin revealed that he was a spy for the Mounties. This caused a big sensation, after people remembered who Claude Morin was. A debate ensued between people who thought it was good for the RCMP to hire Pequiste cabinet ministers to spy and people who thought Pequiste cabinet ministers probably made lousy spies, having spent too many hours whining about federalism to have enough time to learn secret passwords and how to make yellow chalk marks on buildings, along with the other things that great spies have always done.

Mention should be made here — the kindest of all possible mentions — of the Royal Family. The Royal Family has worked hard, travelling to Canada, among other hardships, and all it gets for its trouble is a drooling pack of reporters and would-be book writers lurking behind every lorry with a telephoto lens in order to take pictures of impending divorces.

Worse things happened than that in the People section. If the names Clarence Thomas and Anita Hill, William Kennedy Smith and Mike Tyson mean anything to you, you know it was not a barrel of laughs in Peopleland. It was a better year, all in all, when Gorby was in it and nobody knew he was about to become a consultant.

WALKABOUT—

CUMMINGS, *The Winnipeg Free Press*

DEWAR, *The Ottawa Sun*

"Whats new with familly, Philip?"

"Buckingham Palace? We have Fergle and if you don't pay a million bucks we'll send her back."

KING, *The Ottawa Citizen*

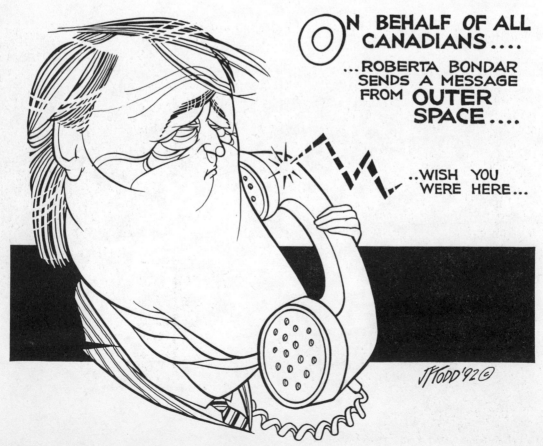

TODD

BADO, *Le Droit*, Ottawa

GABLE, *The Globe and Mail*

Thanks to the Bloc Québécois and other touchy people,
my book is bound to be a bestseller!

PIER, *Le Journal de Montréal*

CUMMINGS, *The Winnipeg Free Press*

AISLIN, *The Gazette / The Toronto Star*

KING, *The Ottawa Citizen*

GABLE, *The Globe and Mail*

"It's Mr Reichmann. Your check for
$750 million is in the mail."

WICKS

ANDY, *Toronto Sun*

MAYES, *The Edmonton Journal*

EDWARDS, *The Whig-Standard*, Kingston

PETERSON, *The Vancouver Sun*

154.

MAYES, *The Edmonton Journal*

PIER, *Le Journal de Montréal*

...the Hockey Fan

GABLE, *The Globe and Mail*

Slices of life in QuébéCan...
(The first in an occasional series)

...EDITORIALISTS WORKING UP A SWEAT OVER LE DOSSIER LINDROS!

AISLIN, *The Gazette / The Toronto Star*

SEBASTIAN

MACKINNON, *The Chronicle-Herald*, Halifax

SEBASTIAN

BLAINE, *The Spectator*, Hamilton

AISLIN, *The Gazette / The Toronto Star*

MALLETTE, *The Financial Post*

CUMMINGS, *The Winnipeg Free Press*

MAYES, *The Edmonton Journal*

SEBASTIAN

LAST FATHER of CONFEDERATION,
JOEY SMALLWOOD, DIES

ALMOST
SYMBOLIC
EH?

SEBASTIAN

BIOGRAPHIES

AISLIN is the name of Terry Mosher's eldest daughter and the "nom de plume" he uses as the editorial page cartoonist for *The Gazette* in Montreal. Syndicated by *The Toronto Star*, he has freelanced in the U.S. and abroad for such publications as *The New York Times*, *Time*, *The National Lampoon*, *Harper's*, *The Atlantic Monthly* and *Punch*. Born in Ottawa in 1941, he is a graduate of Quebec City's École des Beaux-Arts. Aislin has won a number of citations, including Canadian National Newspaper Awards (1977 and 1978), the prestigious Quill Award "...for outstanding contributions to the flow of public information on Canadian affairs," and five individual prizes from the International Salon of Caricature. In May of 1985, Aislin was the youngest person ever to be inducted into the Canadian News Hall of Fame.

Born in 1952 in South Africa, David Anderson, **ANDY** or ERIC, worked for several newspapers in that country. He was the cartoonist for the *Rand Daily Mail* until its closure in 1985 and then for the *Johannesburg Star*. Freelancing in Toronto for the past two years, he still faxes two editorial cartoons a week back to the *Star*.

BADO is Guy Badeaux's last name pronounced phonetically. Born in Montreal in 1949, he worked there for ten years before moving to Ottawa in 1981 to become the editorial page cartoonist for *Le Droit*. Former president of the Association of Canadian Editorial Cartoonists, he won the 1991 National Newspaper Award for political cartooning.

BADO.

JOSH BEUTEL was born in Montreal in 1945. A graduate in Fine Arts from Sir George Williams University (since renamed Concordia), Beutel fell in with the wrong crowd and ended up teaching in Ontario. After stints in various high schools in Ontario and Labrador, all the while freelancing with a few newspapers, Beutel realized he was on the wrong side of education. Before he could become the subject of his students' ridicule, Beutel left teaching for the life of freelance househusbanding. A move to New Brunswick (his wife's home province) and two years of diaper-changing left Beutel ready to handle politics in the Picture Province. In the fall of 1978 he began working for the Saint John *Telegraph-Journal*, and has been toiling ever since for the richest family in the panoply of Canadian megacapitalists; no, not the Reichmanns, the Irvings.

BEUTEL

BLAINE was born in Glace Bay, Nova Scotia. He has been the editorial page cartoonist of *The Spectator* in Hamilton since 1961. Winner of the National Newspaper Award in 1974 and again in 1982, he is the only Canadian cartoonist to win the coveted Reuben Award in New York (1970). First winner of the Grand Prize at Montreal's International Salon of Caricature in 1965, Blaine has also free-lanced for *The New York Times*, *Time* and *Playboy*. A black belt instructor in karate, he also writes music and sings.

Born in Ottawa in 1960, Cameron Cardow (**CAM**) began his career in newspapers at *The Ottawa Citizen* in 1984. In November 1987 he accepted the position of editorial cartoonist at the Regina *Leader-Post*, where he currently draws five cartoons a week. His work appears frequently in other newspapers across Canada.

RICK CEPELLA is a cartoonist living in Nelson, B.C. His cartoons and editorial illustrations have appeared regularly in *The Vancouver Province* and *The Nelson Daily News*. He works summers as a botanical surveyor and art teacher to support his drawing habit.

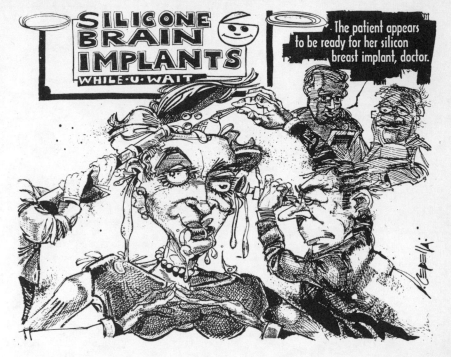

MIKE CONSTABLE was born in Woodstock, Ontario, in 1943. After studying sculpture at the Ontario College of Art, he moved on to Carleton University in Ottawa, where he studied sociology. He was a co-founder of *Guerilla*, a Toronto underground newspaper from 1969 through 1974. In 1977 he was one of the founders of Union Art Services, a co-operative mailing service of graphics and cartoons, which presently goes out to about 45 labour publications. Besides freelancing for *Canadian Tribune*, he is the editor of *Pirahna* (Toronto's National Humour Magazine).

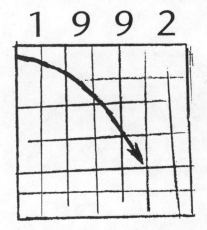

MC

Things are looking up !

Born in Toronto in 1951 with very thick glasses, **PATRICK COR-RIGAN** studied fine arts at the Ontario College of Art. He worked as a freelance illustrator for *The Financial Post*, *Maclean's* and *The Toronto Star*, and joined the *Star* in 1983 as a full-time artist. He now produces one or two editorial cartoons weekly, in addition to illustrations and computer graphics. Winner of several awards (Society of Newspaper Design, 1984; New York Art Directors Club, 1985), he would prefer to work from a Greek island and fax his cartoons home.

PRAISE THE LORD...

AND PASS THE DICE

Born in 1948 in St. Thomas, Ontario, **DALE CUMMINGS** studied animation and illustration at Sheridan College in Oakville. In 1974, he became one of the chief animators in the production of *True North*, the first successful attempt to include animated caricatures in a documentary film on Canadian politics and life. During a brief stay in New York he did some cartoons for *The New York Times*. He returned to Toronto in 1976, where he freelanced for *The Last Post*, *The Canadian Forum*, *Maclean's*, *The Toronto Star*, *Canadian Magazine* and *This Magazine*. Full-time editorial cartoonist with *The Winnipeg Free Press* since 1981, he won the National Newspaper Award in 1983.

Born December 29th, 1958, **FRED CURATOLO** published his first cartoon in *The Toronto Sun* in 1982. Syndicating his work in various dailies, he was staff cartoonist for *The Brampton Guardian* and Metroland newspapers before moving to *The Edmonton Sun* in 1989.

CURATOLO

ANTHONY DELATRI was born in Pennsylvania in 1922 and grew up in rural Quebec, but returned to the U.S. at the age of seventeen to join the army and served overseas during the Second World War. He studied later at the Newark School of Fine and Industrial Art, while drawing for several American publications. During this period, he also tried out as a pitcher for the New York Giants. By the 1950s, he was back in Quebec. He did occasional drawings for *Le Journal de Montréal*, *Montréal-Matin*, and *Dimanche Matin* until becoming the full-time editorial cartoonist for *Le Nouvelliste* in Trois-Rivières in 1967.

Born in Montreal in 1949, **SUSAN DEWAR** attended high school in Toronto, went to the University of Western Ontario in London, and graduated from Toronto Teachers' College. After working in commercial art and cartooning in Toronto, she started her company (Dewar's Ink) freelancing for *Canadian Forum*, *Teen Generation Current* and *The Toronto Sun*. She joined *The Calgary Sun* as full-time editorial cartoonist in 1984 and won the 1987 National Business Writing Award for political cartooning. In October 1988 she moved to Ottawa to become the editorial cartoonist with *The Ottawa Sun*. She is the mother of James Geoffrey.

DEWAR

ANDY DONATO was born in Scarborough in 1937. He graduated from Danforth Technical School in 1955 and began working at Eaton's as a layout artist. He left Eaton's in 1959 to join a small studio and, after a year, decided to freelance. He joined the Toronto *Telegram* in 1961 as a graphic artist working in the promotion department. In 1963 he worked on the redesign of the paper and joined the editorial department. In 1968 he was appointed art director and began cartooning on a part-time basis. After the demise of the *Telegram* he joined *The Toronto Sun* as art director and produced two cartoons a week. In 1974, Donato took over cartooning on a full-time basis. In 1985-86 he served as the second Canadian-born president of the Association of American Editorial Cartoonists.

FRANK A. EDWARDS was born in Belleville, Ontario, in 1940. After graduating from the Ontario College of Art, he worked as a commercial artist for several printing companies. In 1965 Frank accepted a position with Queen's University where he worked for 13 years as a medical illustrator. In 1978 he joined *The Whig Standard* in Kingston as its first full-time cartoonist. His work is syndicated in Canada and the United States.

Born in 1949 in Saskatoon, **BRIAN GABLE** studied fine arts at the University of Saskatchewan. Graduating with a B.Ed. from the University of Toronto in 1971, he taught art in Brockville and began freelancing for the Brockville *Recorder and Times* in 1977. In 1980 he started full-time with the Regina *Leader-Post* and won the National Newspaper Award in 1986. He is presently the editorial cartoonist for *The Globe and Mail*.

Born in Montreal in 1951, and after studies having nothing to do with drawing, Michel Garneau (**GARNOTTE**) has contributed to many newspapers and magazines in Montreal, including *CROC*, *TV Hebdo*, *Protégez-vous* (*Protect Yourself*), *Titanic* (of which he was editor-in-chief), *Les Expos*, *Je me petit-débrouille*, *La Terre de chez nous* and *Nouvelles CSN*, which has carried his cartoons since 1986.

GARNOTTE

Illustrator for the magazine *Voir* since 1987, **ÉRIC GODIN**'s cartoons appear in both its current events and cultural sections. A graphic artist and poster maker for advertising agencies, his work has won numerous national and international awards. He has, since 1983, exhibited in group shows or solo both in Canada and Europe.

Born in Liverpool, England, **GRAHAM HARROP**'s first cartoons appeared in *The Powell River News*. His former jobs include being a copy boy for *The Vancouver Sun*, millworker and taxi driver. He has done freelance cartoons for the Vancouver *Province*, a cartoon strip for the Victoria *Times-Colonist* and he is the author of *Back Bench* in *The Globe and Mail*.

DEWEY PHOTOGRAPHY LTD.

W. A. (Bill) **HOGAN** was born in Montreal, but spent most of his life in Chatham, New Brunswick. He is presently the editorial cartoonist for the Moncton *Times-Transcript*, and he does cartoons for several New Brunswick weeklies. He is the author of the strip *The River Rats* and he has also traveled across the province doing courtroom drawings for CBC TV. Winner of numerous Atlantic Community Newspaper Association Awards and a citation of merit from the Atlantic Journalism Awards in 1989, he has published two collections of his cartoons.

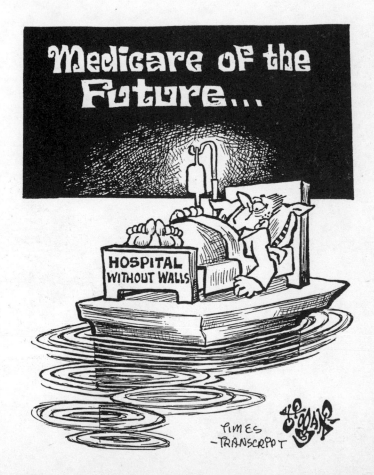

ANTHONY JENKINS was born in Toronto in 1951 and stayed there after graduating from the University of Waterloo and three trips around the world. His work has appeared in *The Globe and Mail* since 1974 and kids Adriana and Zoe have appeared recently.

BRIAN'S MASTERPIECE (WORK IN PROGRESS)

Born in Belfast, Northern Ireland, in 1947, **ALAN KING** came to Canada with his family at the age of two. After graduating in English Literature from the University of Western Ontario, he taught high-school English, and worked as a piano salesman, taxi driver, engineering technician, illustrator and ad agency art director. Having studied classical music as a child and at the university level, he still plays as much piano as he has time for. Father of Christopher, he has been with *The Ottawa Citizen* since 1979.

BOB KRIEGER has been drawing political cartoons for *The Province* since 1981. His work has been published in what may well be the world's largest collection of bathroom books and he is a recent winner of a pair of Bermuda shorts from the Vancouver Press Club.

KRIEGER

Born in 1965, **PAUL LACHINE** lives in Chatham, Ontario, with his wife Deborah and their daughter Katie. Editorial cartoonist and illustrator for the *Chatham Daily News*, he also works for two weekly newspapers and freelances editorial cartoons and illustrations to *The London Free Press* and the Kingston *Whig Standard*.

Born in Sherbrooke, Quebec, in 1963, Ben Lafontaine (**LAF**) graduated in Commercial Arts and slaved a few years in advertising before turning to cartooning, first as a sidewalk caricaturist and now self-syndicated with his Canadian Cartooning Company. His work is distributed to 15 dailies and a dozen weeklies across the country. As well, it is published by *Law Times*, *Labour Times*, *Ottawa Magazine*, *This Magazine* and *Briarpatch*. The Canadian Associates of Labour Media also distributes his cartoons to some 300 union publications. The CCNA gave him the Jasper Award for cartooning in 1987. Ben now lives in Montreal where he is currently working on sculptured caricatures.

Talk about a pathetic political choice...

Born in Swift Current, Saskatchewan, in 1950, **JOHN LARTER** started at *The Lethbridge Herald* in 1974 and went to *The Edmonton Sun* in 1978. He was *The Toronto Star*'s editorial cartoonist from 1980 until he returned west in 1989 to take the same position at *The Calgary Sun*.

SKILL TESTING QUIZ – WHAT DO THESE SPECIES HAVE IN COMMON?

PEREGRINE FALCON

WHITE RHINO

GREY WHALE

CANADIAN FARMER

✱ANSWER (NEAR EXTINCTION.)

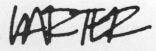

Born in Kitchener, Ontario, in 1964, **JACK LEFCOURT** graduated with a B.A. in fine arts from the University of Waterloo. He started cartooning for the university student paper syndicate in 1985 and has been drawing professionally since 1988. His work is published in about 15 dailies and weeklies across Canada.

Lefcourt

RON LEISHMAN, a fulltime high-school art teacher, free-lances with *The Calgary Herald*, where his cartoons appear once or twice a week. When not involved in these, he can be found doing artwork on his Macintosh computer or spending time with his wife and five children.

· Leishman ·

BRUCE MACKINNON grew up in Antigonish, N.S., studied fine arts at Mount Allison University, and was a member of the Graphic Design program at the Nova Scotia College of Art and Design. He started doing a weekly editorial cartoon with *The Halifax Herald* in 1985, working at home while raising his newborn daughter, Robyn. Through the miracle of day-care, he was able to join the *Herald* on a full-time basis in August of 1986, filling the void left by two-time National Newspaper Award winner, Bob Chambers. He has won several Atlantic Journalism Awards for editorial cartooning, and was named "journalist of the year" in 1991.

...OF COURSE AS WE APPROACHED THE RUNWAY WITH THE LANDING GEAR STILL UP, I TOOK SOME TIME TO REFLECT ON OUR RECENT CUTS TO THE HEALTH CARE SYSTEM HERE IN NEW BRUNSWICK....

PHIL MALLETTE was born in Sault Ste. Marie in 1955, but considers himself a native of Kirkland Lake, Ontario, where he grew up. After graduating from the University of Guelph in 1977 with a Bachelor of Arts degree in Fine Arts, he began working as a freelance cartoonist and illustrator in Toronto. Phil Mallette's cartoons appear daily in *The Financial Post*. His work has also appeared in *The Financial Post Magazine*, *Canadian Business Magazine*, *Toronto Life*, *The Winnipeg Free Press*, *The Globe and Mail* and various other publications.

MALCOLM MAYES was born in Edmonton, Alberta, in 1962. After puberty and some encouragement from cartoonist Yardley Jones, he began to push a pencil on a regular basis. While studying at Grant MacEwan College, he started a company, Mayes Feature Service, to distribute his cartoons to publications across Alberta and has been the editorial cartoonist for *The Edmonton Journal* since June 1986.

Theo Moudakis (**MOU**) was born in Montreal in 1965. He was first hired by *The Chronicle*, a Montreal weekly, in 1983, and since then his work has appeared in most major Canadian dailies as well as *The New York Times*. In January 1991, he left Montreal to become the full-time cartoonist for the Halifax *Daily News*. He is also the Sunday editorial cartoonist for *The Gazette* in Montreal.

A Toronto ad agency production manager, **KEN MUNRO** cartoons on a freelance basis and is a regular contributor to the Union Art Service. He is a graduate of graphic design at George Brown College in Toronto, which fortunately has not hampered his career too much. When not enjoying the many challenges of his profession, he is often found with further challenges on a golf course or a luge track.

DAN MURPHY was born in Missouri. He moved to Canada in the early seventies, drawing for various underground newspapers and aboveground magazines. He currently cartoons for The Vancouver *Province* and the Rothco syndicate.

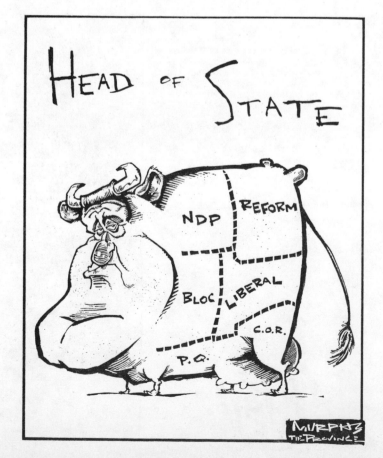

Born in Woodbridge, Ontario, in 1955, **STEVE NEASE** is currently the art director of *The Oakville Beaver*, producing both editorial cartoons and his *Pud* comic strip, which are syndicated by Southam. He is a four times recipient of the (Canadian Community News Association) Jasper Award for cartooning. Nease and his wife Dian have three sons: Robert, Benjamin and Sam.

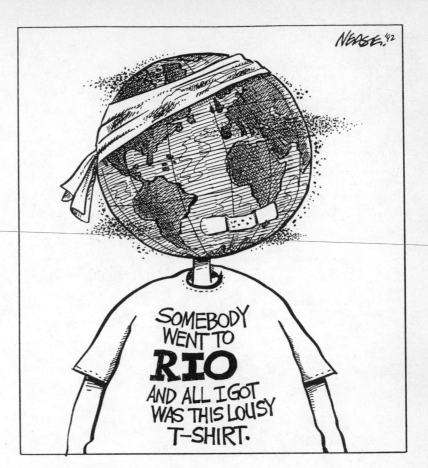

GEOFF OLSON was born in 1959 in Saskatoon. His drawing career began in 1963 with renderings of submarines and houses (Freudians can make of this what they like). Olson has been cartoonist with *The Vancouver Courier* since 1981 and his freelance writing has appeared in publications from *This Magazine* to *The Vancouver Sun*.

Born in Winnipeg in 1936, **ROY PETERSON** works for *The Vancouver Sun* and *Maclean's*. His work has appeared in all major Canadian and most major American newspapers and magazines, as well as *Punch* and *The Spectator* in Britain. He has worked on newspapers, magazines and books as a team with Allan Fotheringham and with Stanley Burke on the bestselling *Frog Fables & Beaver Tales* series. He has illustrated many book covers and produced his own children's book, *The Canadian ABC Book*, as well as a collection of his cartoons, *The World According to Roy Peterson*, and *Drawn & Quartered*, a collection of editorial cartoons pertaining to the Trudeau years, with text by Peter C. Newman. Married with five children, he was, in 1982-83, the first Canadian-born president of the Association of American Editorial Cartoonists. He won the Grand Prize at the International Salon of Caricature in Montreal in 1973 and is three-time winner of the National Newspaper Award.

ROLAND PIER was born in France in 1936. He came to Canada in 1960, traveled extensively, and had various jobs, including construction and working in a gold mine. Arriving in Montreal in 1962, he began freelancing and was eventually hired by *Le Journal de Montréal*. *Le Journal* has since become the largest French-language newspaper in North America. As Pier's cartoons also appear in a sister publication, *Le Journal de Québec*, he is undoubtedly the most widely read cartoonist in Quebec today.

Born in 1935 in Hamilton, Ontario, **DENNY PRITCHARD** worked in auto plants in Ontario and began cartooning as a freelancer in 1975. He was employed as staff cartoonist with *The Saskatoon Star Phoenix* until July 1988 and is now based in Perth, Ontario, where he has resumed his freelance work.

Born July 1st, 1957, in Dunedin, New Zealand, **ADRIAN RAESIDE** got his start in cartooning drawing on the back of bus seats on his way home from school. Moving to Canada in 1972 after a brief period in England, he worked at various jobs, from land surveying on the northern B.C. coast to unloading grain cars in a Thunder Bay grain elevator, before realizing he wasn't much good at any of them. Getting his first break in 1976, illustrating five children's books his mother Joan had written, he quickly became one of the most popular cartoonists on Wildwood Crescent and editorial cartoonist of the Victoria *Times-Colonist* in 1980. As well as being widely syndicated in Canada through his own syndicate, his work also appears in a number of U.S. publications. He has never won an award, and is not president of anything.

INGRID RICE has been in the communication business since 1975, starting out with BCTV, where she worked for the *Noon News Hour*. In 1981 she became art director for *TV Week* and *Westworld* magazines. She started her graphic art company, Ouridea, in 1980 and her illustrations have been used by *The Lumberworker*, BC Transit, the BC Medical Association and other major corporations. She has been associated with *The Vancouver Sun*, contributing editorial cartoons regularly since January 1992. Ingrid spends her free time with her partner and boyfriend taking care of several guinea pigs and a cat.

IRICE

Born in Edmonton in 1946, **VANCE RODEWALT** did advertising cartoons at *The Roughneck* after completing high school. Working for Marvel Comics for five years, he traveled to Europe and, upon his return, began doing political cartoons for the Calgary *Albertan*. When the *Albertan* was bought by *The Calgary Sun*, he remained there for 3 1/2 years before moving on to *The Calgary Herald* where he shared editorial page cartooning duties with Tom Innes. He has assumed full duties since 1987 and has won the 1988 National Newspaper Award for Cartooning. He is also the author of the *Chubb & Chauncey* comic strip.

Since his arrival (from France) in Canada in 1982, **THIERRY SAUER** has had an active career as a storyboard designer for animation and as a comic strip artist. He has many humorous drawings, advertising storyboards, caricatures and illustrations to his credit and is the author and illustrator of *Le droit d'auteur par la bande*. He has been working as editorial page cartoonist for *Le Devoir* since November 1990.

Editorial cartoonist for the *Ottawa Business News*, **FRED SEBASTIAN** was born (in 1964) and bred in Ottawa. A graduate of Algonquin College's Commercial Art/Graphic Design program, his work appears in *Ottawa Magazine*, *Ottawa Business Magazine*, *Legion*, *The Ottawa Citizen*, *The Gazette*, *The Province* and *The Toronto Star*.

TING is the pen name of Merle Tingley, political cartoonist for *The London Free Press*. Born and raised in Montreal, he studied art for one year and then worked briefly as a draughtsman until joining the army at the beginning of the Second World War. He began drawing cartoons on a full-time basis for the *Free Press* in 1948 and received the National Newspaper Award in 1955. He has now retired but still does two drawings a week on a freelance basis.

JIM TODD is a nationally syndicated cartoonist and illustrator with Southam Syndicate and lives in the small southwestern Nova Scotia community of Perotte. He is the winner of the 1990 Atlantic Journalism Award for editorial cartooning.

Since his debut at *The Edmonton Journal* in 1968, **EDD ULUS-CHAK**'s acclaim and popularity have been indisputable. Twice the recipient of the National Newspaper Award for cartooning, he has also won many international awards and prizes. Edd, his wife Susan, their two children and his pet racoon now make their home on five acres of paradise on Gabriola Island, B.C..

"PROBABLY A CABINET APPOINTEE WITH HIS PALTRY BONUS."

Born in London, England, in 1926, **BEN WICKS** claims to have held the Nazis at bay during the war as a swimming pool attendant at a Canterbury army camp. Having learned to play the saxophone in the army, he toured Europe with a band and was later to play in the orchestra on the liner *Queen Elizabeth*. Wicks moved to Canada in 1957, working as a milkman in Calgary. He sold several gag cartoons to *The Saturday Evening Post* and has never looked back. Moving to Toronto in 1960, he produces a daily syndicated cartoon (*Wicks*) and was named to the Order of Canada in 1986.

"Then the birds and the bees got together and caught AIDS."

VINCENT WICKS was born in Calgary in 1959. Leaving school at 18 and travelling through South and Central America before settling down in Canada to become a professional musician, he now draws the syndicated comic strip *The Outcasts*. He is married with two lovely daughters.

Born in Ottawa in 1961, **PETER ZAZULAK** is the editorial cartoonist for the Orleans *Star* and *The Hill Times* (Ottawa). His freelance work appears in various newspapers across Canada. He lives in Gloucester, Ontario, with his wife Virginia and daughter Maxine.

ACKNOWLEDGEMENTS

I would like to thank all the cartoonists involved for making this book possible.

Thanks are also extended to Josh Freed, Susan Girvan, Charles Gordon, Mathilde Hébert, and Matie Molinaro for their invaluable help.

PLUGS

If you've enjoyed this book, here is a list of some of our contributors' current collections:

BEUTEL, *Say Goodnight Frank!*, Non-Entity Press.

CAM & DOLPHIN, R., *Not Politically Correct*, McClelland & Stewart Inc.

RAESIDE, *There Goes the Neighbourhood*, Doubleday Canada.